# Ee

e is for echo
(ECK-OH)

Gg

g is for golf
(GOLF)

h is for hotel
(HOH-TEL)

k is for kilo
(KEY-LOH)

Mm

m is for mike
(MIKE)

n is for november
(NO-VEM-BER)

o is for oscar
(OSS-CAH)

p is for papa
(PAH-PAH)

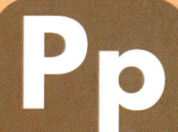

About The Author

Amiel wants to see a world where every human isloved and hopes through the things he creates it helps us get there.

This book is dedicated to Amiel's daughter Lenora.

Check out more of his work on his website at amielbasas.com

First published 2024 by Amiel Basas
Goulburn, Australia
MrAmiel.com

© Copyright 2024 Amiel Basas. All rights reserved.

ISBN 978-0-6486391-2-1

No part of this book may be reproduced, transmitted or stored in an information retrieval system in any form or by any means, graphic, electronic or mechanical, including photocopying, taping, recording or otherwise-except for brief quotations in printed reviews of promotion, without prior written permission from the publisher.

Disclaimer: This book uses AI-generated content using Canva's Magic Media AI tools for the base of the pictures in this book.

Cataloguing in Publishing Data
Title: The Phonetic Alphabet For Kids
Author: Amiel Basas
Subjects: Books & Libraries, School & Education, Reading & Writing, Grammar

A copy of this title is held at the National Library of Australia.

www.ingramcontent.com/pod-product-compliance
Lightning Source LLC
Chambersburg PA
CBRC092341290426
44109CB00009B/176